The Little Book of Economic Myths and Fallacies

By Ken Pruitt

ISBN 978-1-300-78573-6

Table of Contents

Preface to the 2nd Edition

If you purchased the 1st Edition of this book, you will notice some major changes in the 2nd Edition. For starters, the 2nd Edition has a Table of Contents, as well as page numbers. Originally, the book was so short (48 pages), that I didn't feel the need to add a Table of Contents or page numbers, but since new material has been added to the 2nd Edition, as well as certain parts being re-worded (and consequently extended), I decided to go ahead and add the aforementioned items.

New to the book is a section on credit, which I regretfully forgot to add to the 1st Edition, a section dealing with the biggest economic fallacy concerning Immigration, as well as a section dealing with the impact of War on the economy (the subjects of War and Immigration is as political as I'm going to get). Certain parts of the book, such as the section regarding Say's Law, have been drastically re-worded for added clarity.

Foreword

Before I tell you what this book is about, I feel as though I should give a little introduction of myself. My name is Ken Pruitt, and I have been studying economics and economic theory for five years independently. I first started studying economics when I was seventeen; I'm twenty-two now, and I can say without doubt that my studying has fundamentally changed the way I look at the world. In fact, it is my firm belief that everyone should have, at least, a firm foundation in the basics of economic knowledge, and that isn't just my belief. It was also the belief of Ludwig von Mises, arguably the greatest economist of the 20th Century.

Over time, I began having conversations with people; conversations in person, through email, on forums, on the comment sections of YouTube videos, anywhere I could have them. But of course, since I'm not exactly, "In the mainstream," so to speak, I had to have my conversations in the underground, i.e., the areas where people don't generally look to for conversations on economics (or anything of serious substance for that matter).

What I found is an appalling lack of understanding in the field of economics. Ludwig von Mises would roll in his grave if he heard some of the things that I have heard over the course of five years (maybe he did hear them, but I would like to give the people in the academic world back then a little credit, so I'm going to say that he didn't hear the most absurd fallacies and myths being dealt with here). I've also found something else in my conversations, something that has, as far as I'm concerned, achieved axiomatic status, and that is, "Fallacies give birth to more fallacies." Many economic fallacies, from my observation, have their roots in one major misunderstanding (this misunderstanding varies from topic to topic, but it always gives birth to other fallacies). I will attempt to deal with these central fallacies (and a few of their offspring) to the best of my abilities.

I doubt a college professor would find much use for this book (though I could be mistaken). This book is intended for those people who watch the news, listen to pundits, and form their economic/political opinions based on such, and because of this, each section shall be brief (hence the title, "Little Book"). I won't get into politics in this work (with the exception of War and Immigration) because there is no need to. All that needs to be done is to correct these major economic misunderstandings, and your political opinion, assuming you take what you learned from this book and apply it to politics, will change naturally.

With that out of the way, let's get into the first major fallacy/myth of economics.

Economics is for Academics

Whenever you say the word "Economist" to a layman, his mind immediately wanders to the image of a scruffy little professor, wearing a polka-dotted bowtie, in his lab or his classroom working out complex math equations and graphs on his chalkboard. This perception of economists/economics by the general public rests on a serious misunderstanding of what economists do and what economics is. You may not realize it, but you (the layman) use economics every day without thinking about it.

Consider this scenario: it is now the weekend, you're on your knees thanking God that you get a couple of days off after a hard week's work, and you're now figuring out what to do with your weekend. Should you invite your friends over for a game of Poker, or maybe just go out to a club of some sort? Maybe you'd just rather sit at home and watch some TV, or maybe you might decide to take a trip somewhere for the weekend. All of these things entail an opportunity cost; the time you spend playing Poker is time that you won't be able to spend doing something else. The time you spend watching TV is time you can't spend doing something else, etc.

Time, as you see, is a critical factor, not only in our daily lives, but in economics as well.

Also, consider this: suppose you go to the grocery store for some food. What should you get? I don't know, that's up to you. You could get milk, eggs, steak, hamburger meat, and bread. But, someone else may not like those things, so instead, they decide to get something else.

There are two things to keep in mind; first, the value that you place on the items you buy, or considering to buy is purely subjective, in other words, they only apply to you and not to anyone else. If you see a steak on the shelf for $5, and you decide that, presently, that steak isn't worth $5, you won't buy it. If someone buys a steak for $5, then they've made the decision that, presently, the steak is worth more to them than the $5, and this makes the trade possible.

So, if someone buys bread for $3, and you hear them complain, "This bread ain't worth $3," you can ask them point-blank, "Then why did you buy that bread for $3, jackass?"

Secondly; whatever you choose to buy at the grocery store, the money you spend buying whatever you buy is money that will not/cannot be spent elsewhere.

If you spend $4 on a gallon of milk, that is $4 that you can't spend elsewhere. Everyone takes this into account, in one way or another.

Now, that brings us to our next problem: how likely are you to buy items you already have, as compared to before when you didn't have those same items?

You can, but the odds aren't good that you will. From this we can see that, the more you have of something (all other things equal), the less that something is worth to you. If you see a steak on the rack for $5, would you pay $5 for that steak when you already have two of them sitting in the freezer? But, suppose the price went down to $3 for the same steak. Would you buy that steak then, even though you have two of the same steaks sitting in the freezer? What if it went down to $2? Eventually, you would cave in and buy the steak, even though you have two of those same steaks sitting in the freezer.

This is called Supply and Demand in the economic world. If Supply goes up, and Demand remains the same or decreases, prices will fall. If Supply goes down, and Demand remains the same or rises, prices will rise. If Demand rises, and Supply remains the same or decreases, then prices will rise. If Supply and Demand are rising at the same time, then, all other things equal, the price won't change.

Just from analyzing two typical scenarios, we see very key principles of economics at work. First, time and resources are scarce.

Secondly, value is subjective. Thirdly, we see the principle of Supply and Demand (a function of subjective value) at work.

To sum this up in the words of Ludwig von Mises, "Economics must not be relegated to classrooms and statistical offices and must not be left to esoteric circles. It is the philosophy of human life and action and concerns everybody and everything. It is the pith of civilization and of man's human existence."[1]

Fallacies Concerning the Above Principles

These principles seem so easy to understand, but you would be surprised how many people (most of them are would-be professional economists) misunderstand and misinterpret them. These misinterpretations/misunderstandings have lead not only to the most persistent, plausible fallacies to grace the human mind with their presence, but also to the most absurd fallacies that are dealt with here. Some of the fallacies (or at least one in particular) are so absurd, it seems like a miracle that anyone would propose them.

Let's start with what I consider to be the most persistent economic fallacy in the history of man. A few professional economists may be thinking, "The Broken Window Fallacy!" but that is coming a little later. Right now, we're going to deal with an even bigger fallacy.

Demand is Prior to Supply

This is a fallacy of the highest caliber. Not only is it easy to make, it's hard to understand exactly why this is a fallacy. The Demand is Prior fallacy goes like this, "There is a greater supply of goods and services because there is a demand for those services. If there were no demand for these goods and services, they just wouldn't exist. Demand, therefore, creates supply, and a good economic policy should be to encourage demand."

First, they've totally misunderstood what **Demand** is. Demand is not mere human want. Wants (human desires) are infinite, means (resources such as land, labor, time, and money) are scarce. Demand is measured in the amount of actual purchases made. If I stand outside of an Apple store staring at the iPad, that isn't Demand, that's mere want. If this can safely be considered to be Demand, then we would never have a problem of lack of Demand, as many would-be economists would have us believe is the case. This is why many would-be economists talk about "Stimulating Aggregate Demand." This means that we should have an economic policy that encourages people on the whole to spend more money, thereby growing business, thereby growing the economy.

The problem with this is the fact that Demand in and of itself doesn't create Supply, but in fact a synergetic combination of Supply and Demand is what creates Supply.

13

To show you what I mean, consider this; suppose you have a simple shoemaker. He makes and sells shoes, collects his wages, and then spends his income in the neighboring shops.

The people who put forth this particular fallacy would be quick to interject, "Yes, but the fact that the shoemaker is able to be employed in the first place is because of the fact that there is a Demand for shoes. If people didn't want shoes, the shoemaker would be out of business."

But, in interjecting in this fashion, they avoid altogether a very critical question, namely, "Could society at large have Demanded (purchased) those shoes had there been no Supply of shoes?"

The person would interject again, "No, they couldn't have **purchased** those shoes, but the fact people **want** shoes is what allowed them to come into existence." Notice here that the confusion between **Want** and **Demand** is manifestly apparent. Just as a side note, many would-be economists call the purchases themselves, "Effective Demand." I shall only quote Henry Hazlitt on the issue of Effective Demand.

"The whole term "effective demand" is today either nonsensical or confusing anyway. Modern economists do not need the adjective "effective" in front of "demand." Demand is effective by definition. If it is not effective, it is not called demand but need, desire, wish, or longing. The word "demand" implies the requisite desire along with the requisite purchasing power."[2]

Now, on occasion, it is true that there is prior want for a new product, but this isn't always true. Take, for example, the Personal Computer. Was there a prior want (or Demand) for the Personal Computer? Hardly. The want for Personal Computers had to be created, and it was created by the person/persons responsible for making the Personal Computer attractive enough for people to spend their hard-earned money on it. Or, to take a more recent example, consider the iPad. Was there a prior want or Demand for the iPad?

Not at all. In fact, prior to the iPad, the tablet computer was thought to be an item of science-fiction, and the same is true for the Personal Computer.

To return to our example of the shoemaker, yes it is true that the Demand (purchases) of the shoemaker's shoes will grant him income that he can spend in the neighboring shops, but here is the problem; even though the shoemaker is paying in the local currency at the neighboring shops, he is ultimately paying in shoes. How can that be, you ask? To answer that question, you only need to ask, "Could the people at large Demand (purchase) the shoes the shoemaker sells, and in turn provide him the income that he spends in the neighboring shops, had those shoes not existed?"

15

The purchasing power of the shoemaker depends, it is true, on Demand (purchases) for shoes, but the ability for the public to Demand (purchase) shoes depends first and foremost on the existence of shoes. The shoes that the shoemaker provides is what, ultimately, pays for whatever goods/services he buys from the neighboring shops, for if he didn't provide those shoes or something in place of the shoes, the only means he would have to acquire the goods and services the neighboring shops offer would be theft.

Even though the shoemaker, in the short-run, is paying for the goods and services offered by the neighboring shops in the local currency, he is ultimately paying for those goods and services in the shoes that he provides for the people at large to purchase.

This is called, "Say's Law" in the economic world, named after French businessman and economist, Jean-Baptiste Say, though many would-be economists today (quite wrongfully) reject this as being debunked.[3]

It is also very important to note that this shouldn't be misunderstood as, "Supply creates Demand." This is a simplification that doesn't correctly describe Say's Law. A much better simplification is, "Supply creates the **possibility** of Demand."

We see from all this that Demand is not prior to Supply, neither is it true that Supply is prior to Demand. Supply and Demand are equal, synergetic principles, and they must be treated as such. But this creates one more problem that has to be dealt with, namely, how can they be treated as both? When the government intervenes, they must by necessity favor one or the other, i.e., Supply or Demand.

The government can't, due to the nature in which the government derives its income and its power, favor both Demand and Supply at the same time through intervention. When the government intervenes, it always intervenes on the part of either the Suppliers, or the Consumers. It is neither politically feasible, nor is it possible logically, for the government to intervene on the behalf of both the Consumers, and the Suppliers at the same time.

By intervening in this manner, they off-set the synergy between Supply and Demand by making one artificially higher than the other would otherwise permit, and as a result, severe imbalances ensue.

The only way, ironically, for the government to favor both is to favor neither. The government and the people at large must realize that because Supply and Demand are in fact equal, synergetic principles, Supply and Demand adjust themselves to each other accordingly.

The Demand is Prior fallacy gives birth to several other fallacies, but for now, I shall only address the one which I mentioned earlier, and it happens to be the biggest fallacy to spawn from the fallacy we just addressed.

a. The Broken Window Fallacy

The Broken Window Fallacy is, notoriously, one of the most persistent fallacies to plague the economic world. It is often said that there are no sure things in life besides death and taxes, but I disagree. It is a sure thing that whenever a disaster happens, be it war, a hurricane, an earthquake, etc., you're going to have someone (most likely a professional economist) spewing this fallacy. It goes like this. Suppose you have a bakery sitting on the street corner on some city block. All of a sudden, some kid comes along and throws a rock through it, breaking the baker's window. The baker comes out and is mad as hell because his window has been broken and he has to pay the glazier (glass maker) to come fix it.

The crowd that gathered around to see the spectacle sees one of its members say, "Wait, this isn't a bad thing. Think about it. The money that the baker gives to the glass maker will go to maybe a tailor, who will then spend money at the butchery, who will then buy a new pair of shoes from the shoemaker, etc. So therefore, this will create jobs and help the economy, and we owe the kid that broke this window an incalculable debt."

This fallacy has a mainstream manifestation in the form of an article written by Paul Krugman, Nobel Prize-Winning Economist in the New York Times on September 14th, 2001, in the wake of the 9/11 terror attack.

"It seems almost in bad taste to talk about dollars and cents after an act of mass murder. Nonetheless, we must ask about the economic aftershocks from Tuesday's horror.

These aftershocks need not be major. **Ghastly as it may seem to say this, the terror attack -- like the original day of infamy, which brought an end to the Great Depression -- could even do some economic good.** But there are already ominous indications that some will see this tragedy not as an occasion for true national unity, but as an opportunity for political profiteering."

Krugman continues in the same article: "So the direct economic impact of the attacks will probably not be that bad. **And there will, potentially, be two favorable effects.**

First, the driving force behind the economic slowdown has been a plunge in business investment. Now, all of a sudden, we need some new office buildings. As I've already indicated, the destruction isn't big compared with the economy, **but rebuilding will generate at least some increase in business spending.**

Second, the attack opens the door to some sensible recession-fighting measures. For the last few weeks there has been a heated debate among liberals over whether to advocate the classic Keynesian response to economic slowdown, a temporary burst of public spending. There were plausible economic arguments in favor of such a move, but it was questionable whether Congress could agree on how to spend the money in time to be of any use -- and there was also the certainty that conservatives would refuse to accept any such move unless it were tied to another round of irresponsible long-term tax cuts. **Now it seems that we will indeed get a quick burst of public spending, however tragic the reasons."**

This is tied to The Broken Window Fallacy. Returning to our example of the baker and his broken window. It is true that the glazier will come, replace the window for a set sum, and be on his way. He will in turn spend his income with other people who will spend that income on something else. Indeed, this is true and there is no problem with this as stated. The problem is that we don't see what the baker would've done with this sum of money had he not had to pay the glazier to come fix his window in the first place.

The baker may have invested that sum in his business and thus would've been more productive, or maybe he would've gotten a new pair of shoes from the shoemaker, or maybe he would've bought a new book from the bookstore, etc. The same set of opportunities are being created without the destruction of the glass window. Indeed, if we factor this in, then society on the whole has suffered a net loss of one window.

The same is true for the 9/11 Terror Attacks, only in the case of the latter, society as a whole has suffered the net loss not only of three buildings, but also of 3,000 lives. If it is true that this type of destruction creates prosperity, then we should just riot. We should just have a massive riot, destroying all of the property we can, kill each other off as best we can, and then we should pay to have it all rebuilt and replaced, and for the funerals that'll have to be had for all of the people killed, because after all, that'll create jobs... right?

Professor Krugman's fundamental misunderstanding is readily apparent. He doesn't understand that Demand, on its own merits, doesn't create Supply. If it were in fact true that Demand, in the sense that Krugman and many others understand the term, creates Supply, then we would never have a problem of scarcity.

Now, a very popular critique of this among many would-be economists is that this assumes full employment, and that since we don't have full employment, The Broken Window creates jobs and this critique of it is wrong. The problem with this is two-fold.

First, what the hell do they mean by Full Employment? Secondly, why in the world would we want Full Employment (assuming the literal meaning of the term here) to begin with? Human values are constantly changing, as reflected in the market prices (assuming they're unhampered). When resources make a transition from one use to another, they must first become idle (which is, ironically, a use in and of itself). This allows the market to make the necessary adjustments needed to fully employ those resources at a later date.

Full Employment would make it much harder (if not impossible) for resources to shift to different uses, and thereby, creating an economy where nothing changes (which would implode in on itself eventually).

But many would-be economists today say that having idle resources is a bad thing. We don't want to have idle resources, they say. All resources need to be used to their most productive capacity at all times. The problem here is that resources are much more productive when they're idle than when they're spent on inefficient production purposes carried out through government management/stimulus in the name of; job creation, stimulating aggregate demand, etc. Idle resources are absolutely essential for a market to function.

So when you hear some pundit or some would-be economist saying that the unhampered market doesn't create Full Employment, please point out to them and your peers than the entire concept of Full Employment is silly.

In the words of Frédéric Bastiat, "There is only one thing that separates a good economist from a bad. The bad economist takes into account only that which is seen. The good economist takes into account that which is seen and that which is not seen."

Roughly 80% of all economic fallacies can be avoided by taking this into account.

On the Issue of Money

Money is something we use every day, but as a whole, we know very little about. We've used it for so many years, we couldn't think about using something else, but we did at one point in time. In order to address the fallacies that many people make regarding money, and they are numerous (too numerous to cover in this work), we need to ask the historical question, "Where did money begin? Why did we start using money?"

Before we had money, we had something called the Barter System. The Barter System is pretty easy to understand, and is still practiced today in some instances. If you have a horse, and you trade it to someone for a cow, that's Barter. You are directly exchanging your goods for someone else's. But Barter has serious limits, one of them is called, "The Double Coincidence of Wants." This means that if you have a horse, and someone else has a cow, neither of you can make the exchange because neither trader wants what the other person is trading.

Now, if the trader who has the horse thought about it for a moment, he could easily solve this problem. He could trade his horse for something else, not because he wants that something else personally, but because he wants to trade it for the cow. This method of exchange is called Indirect Exchange, and it solves the problem of "The Double Coincidence of Wants."

Barter has yet another problem, and that problem is of indivisible goods. Suppose you have a rake; can you exchange that rake for clothes, water, and a little bit of food? Of course not, because you would have to split the rake into three or more pieces, and then the rake would be useless.

Well, over time, with hundreds of thousands of people using the Indirect Exchange method, certain "mediums" have emerged as mediums of exchange. These "mediums" have been, rocks, copper, iron, gold, silver, salt, tobacco, just to name a few. All of these commodities have been money at one point, and it is with this we see what money is and where it came from. Money is a medium of exchange that evolves over time from the transactions of hundreds of thousands of acting individuals.

Contrary to popular myth, money didn't come from some academic, or some political official, or from some central banker, as Paul Krugman and others would have us believe. Money was created by the market.

What makes money so complicated to deal with in this type of work is not only its origins, but its status as the medium of exchange. This has created some serious economic fallacies. We'll start with the big one, and work our way down.

a. We Need Government to Create and Manage Money

I told you that we're starting with the big one (LOL!) Well, since we've laid out the origins of money, we have a reasonable foundation to work with, and we're prepared to ask the painfully obvious question, "If the government didn't create money to begin with, why do we need the government to create and manage money now?"

The answer is, we don't. But this question has a critically-flawed assumption built into it that must be dealt with, and that assumption is that money can actually be created by the government. This is not true. The government can put the faces of Kings and Presidents on gold/silver/copper/iron coins, but those precious metals were already money prior to the government coining them. What about the paper money that is used today? It is true that the market experimented with paper money, or fiat money as it is more appropriately called, but the market quickly rejected this form of money as unreliable, and it isn't hard to see why.

The market, when it is allowed to have real choice over the currency used, will always choose some sort of commodity money (gold, silver, copper, iron, or some other commodity to be used as a medium of exchange) over paper currency.

Consider this; take a dollar bill (any will do), and read what it says on it. It says, "Federal Reserve Note." The Federal Reserve is the central bank of the United States currently as of October 30, 2012, and what they mean by "Federal Reserve Note" is that the paper money you carry now is actually a promissory note (basically an I.O.U) from the Federal Reserve (or the Fed as it is commonly called) to pay the amount listed. The amount of what, you ask? That's just it. The only thing these I.O.U.s are linked to is deposits holding, you guessed it, more dollars. In other words, that promissory note isn't backed by anything solid like commodities, and has nothing to vouch for it except the full faith and credit of the U.S government, but in this is a serious problem.

Never mind the past conduct of the United States government. In this instance, even if it has maintained full credit (kept all of its promises to everyone it ever made a promise to) through-out its entire existence, on this it has absolutely no credibility, nor can it ever have any sort of credibility. The government simply cannot, no matter how hard it tries, replicate a product which was the result of an astronomical number of exchanges over thousands of years. The absolute best that a government can "create" (in the strict sense of the term) regarding money is a voucher, but what is a voucher at its core besides a claim against some type of debt?

The Dollar, the currency of the United States, is precisely that; a voucher, i.e., it is debt-based. Real money, i.e., commodity money, is not a claim against anything (it isn't a voucher), and at its core, it is nothing more than a simple medium to facilitate exchange. The most important feature of commodity money, aside from it being impossible to manipulate by the government, is the fact that unlike a voucher, it isn't based in debt.

The government, therefore, cannot create money, in the true sense of the term, they can only create debt.

There is yet another problem with government managing of the money supply. Even if you accept the idea of the government actively managing the money supply, increasing it/decreasing it whenever they see fit, how can they possibly know how much money should be circulating through the economy?

It's not like they don't have the resources to know such a thing. After all, the government has the world's greatest bankers, mathematicians, and economists at their disposal working around the clock on this problem. They should be able to figure this out... right?

Wrong. The population is estimated to be 300,000,000 in the United States alone. Mathematically, that equals an exponentially higher number in terms of exchange possibilities. Even if the government got lucky and found the right equations, they wouldn't be good for longer than a day, and it would've been nothing but a stroke of luck that they found those equations in the first place. Once they find the right equations, they would have to be changed, from the ground up, every single day, which is a self-defeating purpose because that means that they would have to change thousands upon thousands of equations every day from the ground up, and of course, this process would take longer than a day.

There is also a very deadly assumption built into the idea that the government should manage the money supply, and that assumption is that the government can plan the entire nation's finances, when it just can't.

To drive this point home further, consider this very simple equation.

$$f(x) = 5x + 3$$

In this equation, 5 and 3 are constants. This in and of itself is a problem because, in economic activity, there are no constants; all value is subjective and people's values are constantly changing (arguably, the only true constant in economics).

So in order for me to be able to work with this equation at all, it would have to be re-written as

$$f(x) = ax + b$$

But, this has its own set of problems. In order for me to work with this equation, I would have to assume a constant, but if I'm just assuming constants, then I'm running equations in the dark and the whole thing has about as much serious meaning as tits on a bull.

There is one final problem to deal with in regards to paper currencies; they can be created at will. If you're running low of money, you can just fire up the printing presses and create more money, but this makes the currency fundamentally worthless, and the less the currency is worth, the higher prices are going to be.

Money has purchasing power precisely because it is scarce, and it is desired.

b. Money is not an item of Supply and Demand

This has got to be, hands down, the most absurd statement that I've ever heard within economic discussion and I challenge someone to find me something sillier and more ridiculous than this. I said earlier that there were statements in this book that would make Ludwig von Mises roll in his grave. Well, this isn't one of them. In fact, this statement is so absurd, Mises would not just roll in his grave, he would rise from the grave as a zombie, write a lengthy scholarly article on why this is nonsense, then he would hunt down the person who said this and eat his brains. This is pure absurdity, not only because it is easy to see through, but because it is particularly easy to avoid.

Throughout my time studying economics, I've had many discussions, and this fallacy had reared its ugly head more than once. This fallacy is centered on the fact that money is a medium of exchange... which is baffling because that's one of the things that would tell you that this is nonsense. This line of thought goes like this, "Money is the medium of exchange, and as such, it doesn't exist in the realm of Supply and Demand."

I pointed out in response that, if money weren't an item of supply or demand, it wouldn't be traded on any level. He retorted, with what has to be, the most contradictory statement I've ever seen anyone make.

"Sure, there is a supply of, and a demand for, money, but because money is the medium of exchange, money can't exist in the realm of Supply and Demand."

Do you see the contradiction here? There is a Supply of, and a Demand for, X Commodity, oh but it doesn't exist in the realm of Supply and Demand... to make matters worse, someone else chimed in and demanded that I either produce the mathematical equation that PROVES money exists in the realm of Supply and Demand, or in his words, "stfu."

Well, I can't produce a mathematical equation, so logic will have to suffice here. We've already seen how money comes into existence, and that alone proves that this idea is garbage, but let's go deeper.

A while back, I sold my iPod Classic to my neighbor as a favor to him for $70. From the buyer's (my neighbor's) perspective, the money is his Supply and my iPod is his Demand, and from the perspective of the seller (myself), the money is the Demand and the iPod is my Supply. The person putting this fallacy forward said in response to this, "No, the iPod is your neighbor's supply," but this can't be because he is not, before the transaction is made, in any way, the owner of the iPod in question.

In order for you to call something your Supply, you have to have some means of disposal over the something in question (whatever the hell that something is). In the example of my friend buying an iPod from me, he has no means of disposal over the iPod in question until the transaction is made, and cannot, therefore, be considered to be his Supply. Bear in mind that all of this is ignoring a severe logical absurdity, namely, **that this would mean that the iPod would be both my neighbor's Supply and Demand at the same time before even buying it!**

c. All Money is Debt

This is a fallacy that is very easy to fall into, and is put forth mainly by Zeitgeist advocates (I won't go into what Zeitgeist is here. That would be writing a book within a book). Their understanding of money is fundamentally flawed, as the history of money (covered earlier) shows, but there is a nugget of truth to it in that it applies quite perfectly to paper (fiat) money.

Their error then is readily apparent: they don't understand the history of money. As a side note, when I pointed out to Zeitgeist advocates that paper currency isn't money and that only commodities such as Gold and Silver can be money (I am a Gold-Back), one of them replied, "The only way your precious gold can be money is if it's put into a bank and then loaned out at interest."

I never did reply back to this, as I had grown weary of having exchanges with Zeitgeist advocates. You'd be spending your time more productively by bashing your head against a brick wall than talking with those people. Again, we know from the history of money that this is silly, but let's address this anyway.

You mean to tell me, that the only way Gold can be money is if it is deposited into a bank and then loaned out at interest?

Ok, but why mine Gold in the first place? It clearly has some sort of value or there wouldn't have been any Gold miners. Also, we know from history that Gold has been money for no less than 6,000 years, and this pre-dates the earliest recorded banks in history by no less than 2,000 years. To top this off, banks didn't start accepting money deposits until the days of the Roman Empire.

So, if there were no banks during the time Gold was a medium of exchange, how did Gold come to be used as money?

This understanding of money runs rampant throughout the Zeitgeist camp, but it is a non-sequitor (i.e., the logic doesn't follow through).

All of this can be verified with a quick Google Search.

d. Money Doesn't Produce Anything

This is yet another easy fallacy to fall into, but once you consider a world without money, this is easily seen as a fallacy. We know, once again from the history of money which we dealt with earlier, that money came about as an evolution of Indirect Exchange, but we didn't cover one of the major benefits of money, namely, that the existence of money allows for specialization in the labor force. This means that people can specialize in a given trade and be more productive than if they had to barter for the sole reason that, no matter what they specialize in, they can always be confident that they can sell their goods and services for the money currently being used.

Without money, a person would have to be proficient in more than one trade to be secure in his future. It is from this that we see quite clearly what money produces. Because money produces trading opportunities that would otherwise not exist, money allows for specialization of the labor force, and a greater efficiency in the division of labor.

The "Money Doesn't Produce Anything" fallacy is primarily put forth by the Zeitgeist advocates.

All of these fallacies regarding money stem from not knowing how money came to be used in the first place. Now that you know this information, you won't fall for these fallacies.

What is Credit?

I ask this question because, like money, very few people understand what credit is. Consider this; suppose someone decides one day that they want to start a small-business that deals with computers. Once he calculates his expenses, he estimates that to start his business on a strong foundation, he needs $10,000 more than he currently has. After considering the pros and cons, he decides to go to the bank to request a small-business loan for the amount in question.

Now, if the banker is impressed enough with the entrepreneur's presentation to give him the loan, would you be inclined to say that the bank gave the entrepreneur the credit he needed to open his business?

If you said yes, then you don't know what credit is. It is a common misconception that credit is something a banker gives to a borrower, but this isn't true. Credit is something that you already have, either because you have marketable assets that are worth more than the loan in question, and/or you've proven yourself to be an honest borrower who is reliable when it comes time to repay the loan.

If the banker decides of his own free will to grant a borrower a loan, it is precisely because he feels confident that he will be repaid the principle plus the agreed upon rate of interest.

So, returning to our example of the entrepreneur who wants to start a small business. If the banker decides to grant him the $10,000 loan (just for the sake of the example, we'll assume an interest rate of 25%), it will be because the banker feels sure that he can collect $12,250 at a later date. In other words, the banker feels that, for whatever reason, the entrepreneur in question has enough credit to his name to warrant loaning him $10,000 for his business project.

It is important to remember that, from the perspective of the borrower, credit and debt are the same thing. If someone says that they need more credit, what they are really saying is that they need more debt. But you'll never hear a pundit or a politician say such a thing.

In the current state of affairs, people such as President Obama are right when they say that credit is the life-blood of the economy, but the very fact that they are right when they say this is the economic problem that has to be dealt with. Why in the world would consumers and businesses going into perpetual debt be the life-blood of the economy?

With that, we're ready to deal with some common fallacies concerning credit

a. We Need to Make Credit Easy to Obtain

This fallacy is put forth primary by the "Progressives," and it basically goes like this. "Credit is absolutely essential to the economy. Small businesses need it in order to pay their salaries, and to expand and to increase production. Therefore, the easier credit is to obtain, the easier it will be for small businesses to expand, hire more workers, and it will even have the added effect of making it easier for other people to become entrepreneurs and to become small business owners."

There are several logical fallacies here. First of all, they have forgotten one crucial fact that was covered earlier in the book, namely, that resources are scarce. Returning to our entrepreneur looking to opening a small-business dealing in computers, the $10,000 that the bank loans him is, by logical necessity, $10,000 that can't be loaned out to someone else.

If credit is made to be easy to obtain (in the sense that they are using the term easy), then, by logical necessity, loans will inevitably be made to would-be entrepreneurs who're not competent enough to use those funds to their fullest potential, i.e., they won't be able to run a business profitably.

Easy-credit policies always lead to speculative scandals down the road, and those speculative scandals are always followed by calls for government regulation/supervision of the lending industry.

The second fallacy stems from the fact that, again, from the borrower's perspective, credit and debt are the same thing. If businesses need to go into debt in order to pay salaries, then it follows that, for whatever reason, they are not bringing in enough revenue to pay their expenses. Now, maybe this is a temporary slump. All businesses I'm sure have experienced this at least once in their lifetime, but, **the people who put forth this fallacy want this to be able to continue indefinitely if they feel that it needs to!**

The problem is, that because resources are scarce, there is no way for this to continue indefinitely no matter how much credit you can create out of thin air. That easy credit is ultimately paid for, one way or another, and easy credit always costs more in the long run than tight credit does in the short-run.

But, to drive this point home further, let's take a hypothetical case and assume that resources (excluding time) are infinite. Can this continue indefinitely now that we have infinite resources?

Not only can it not continue even if you had infinite resources, other production processes couldn't even start. Since resources are infinite, there would be absolutely no incentive to work (because, you know, resources are just so abundant). Those businesses that were in place that needed credit/debt to pay their expenses will end up shutting down anyway, despite the central effort to keep them open, because of the fact that when resources are infinite, it again becomes a question of incentives. What incentive is there to engage in labor each day for a wage when resources are infinite?

In other words, why would people bother to produce when they already have all of the resources they will ever need in their lifetime, and then some?

But, let's grant our opponent their inevitable objection to this and let's assume that with infinite resources, there is an incentive to work (don't ask me how the hell that's possible, let's just run with this for a moment and see where it takes us).

Then, in this case, we arrive at a very silly conclusion, namely, that resources would end up being over-allocated. This is silly because an over-allocation of resources in a world with infinite resources is strictly impossible, but if you follow the logic, this is where it takes us. The point of the hypothetical is to show you that this process of endless easy credit in order to keep businesses open can't even work in a scenario where resources are infinite, and **yet this is expected to work in a world made up entirely of scarce resources!**

Taxes

This is a source of many confusions among voters and layman alike. Many a fallacy in this category comes from, you guessed it, a lack of understanding regarding the nature of taxation, what determines revenue, etc. For instance, it is generally thought that the tax rate is the main factor, but there is a problem with this in that the tax rate is only one major factor that determines tax revenue. In fact, there are three major factors that determine tax revenue. The first is, quite obviously, the tax rate itself. If you set the rate too high, you're not going to get enough revenue, and if you set the rate too low, you're not going to get enough revenue. I shall return to this later.

The second factor is how well the tax code is enforced. The more lengthy and complicated a tax code is, the harder it will be to adequately enforce the tax code, and thereby, the revenues you do collect will suffer.

The third factor, the one that is frequently overlooked, is the employment rate of the people at large. The less employment you have, the less revenue will be collected.

With these things in mind, it is pretty obvious that our tax system is incredibly inept, and no one will deny this. But what should be done about it? This is where we start running into problems.

On the one hand, we have the "Tax the Rich" crowd. These people believe that the rich aren't paying their "fair share" (the term "fair share" couldn't be vaguer than it is) in taxes, and that they should be taxed more.

Let's ignore the statistically apparent fact that the rich already pay 70% of the taxes the government collects for a moment[4], let's deal with the logical problem here.

When we're talking about the really rich, the "1%" as their commonly called today, we never seem to ask the question, "How did they get rich?" It is true that some people inherit wealth from their really rich parents, but if they aren't worthy of that wealth, it doesn't stay with them very long. They either spend that wealth wastefully, or they are suckered into investing into terrible businesses that shouldn't receive funds. Hence the old wise saying, "A fool and his money are soon parted."

In fact, the very nature of big business is to serve the many. Those businesses that cater to the special tastes of the rich never outgrow medium or even small size. The rich became rich precisely because they invested in land, labor, and capital, and used them to create wealth for everyone in the form of goods/services that the public at large wants, and in doing so, they also created wealth in the form of jobs for the unemployed. When this is considered, it is quite obvious that the rich pay more than their "fair share" of taxes.

On the other hand, we have the people who say that all tax cuts pay for themselves, and they point to The Laffer Curve to prove this. It is mostly Mainstream Republicans/ Reaganites who put forth this fallacy.

First of all, The Laffer Curve doesn't say that all tax cuts pay for themselves, it simply says that if you set the tax too high, you won't collect as much revenue as if you set it lower.

Here's an example; if you had the personal income tax rate set at 70%, and lowered the income tax rate after ten years to 40%, you would see an increase in revenue, not because tax cuts pay for themselves, but because lowering the tax puts you on the optimum side (the upward-sloping side) of the curve.

With that, we are ready to deal with a few of the fallacies associated with taxation.

a. We Should Tax the Rich to Increase Revenue

This is a fallacy that is easy to fall into, but with a little bit of economic reasoning, it is easily exploded. This fallacy is put forth primarily by the group of people who call themselves, "Progressives."

The line of thought goes like this, "The rich make much more money than the middle/poor working class, and we must have public spending to provide certain services (especially for the poor) that the market can't provide, but those vital services have gotten to be more expensive, and thus in order to provide these vital services for the middle/poor class, as well as start paying off the national debt, we have to increase taxes on the rich."

First and foremost, they're falling into the trap of thinking that the tax rate is the only real factor with regards to tax revenue, when as I have shown, there are three major factors that determine tax revenue.

Secondly, they fail to consider something else, which is, that all of the money that the poor/middle class are paying in personal income tax is coming from salaries paid out by the wealthy for goods/services rendered. When this is considered, it is not hard to see that all of the tax revenue collected, ultimately, comes from the wealthy in the first place.

But, what about the proposed increases in revenue that this would supposedly bring? Isn't that worth raising taxes on the rich? First, assuming you actually get those revenue increases, the businesses in question would merely pass this added expense onto the consumer, and there are a few ways that this can be done.

First, the wages of the employees of those companies can be cut.

Secondly, they can increase the prices of their goods and services.

Thirdly, they can lay off employees, which will cost the tax payers because now they have to pick up the tab for more unemployment benefits being paid out.

Corporations usually do a combination of the above in order to mitigate expenses such as minimum wage, compliance with government regulations, and taxation.

This shows you that, even if you manage to get the proposed revenue increases (though it is highly unlikely that you will), it won't mean anything because the corporation doesn't directly pay this tax; they pass these expenses onto the consumer/taxpayer, and sometimes even the employee (if he's one of those unfortunate souls who gets laid off because of this nonsense).

The result is less jobs, and a poorer standard of living for the poor/middle class, while the rich maintain their profits.

This is why political/social commentators such as Ed Schultz and Cenk Uygur can look at our economy and blame the rich (or the 1% as they're commonly called today) for all of our problems.

They see corporate profits sky-high, they see massive lay-offs (which they quite wrongfully attribute to greed and "mean-spiritedness") but they don't see past that.

They don't see that corporations pass all involuntary expenses, i.e., minimum wage, taxes, adherence to various other regulations, etc., to the consumer/taxpayer.

The central mistake that the "Progressives" make when they advocate taxing the rich to increase revenue (and it is the same mistake that makes them cling to this fallacy as if their life depended on it) is that they believe the extra revenue (again, assuming they actually get that revenue) will come out of excessive corporate profits. But in reality, the person who will ultimately be responsible for this tax is the average man, in his capacity as a consumer (higher prices for goods and services), as a taxpayer (more taxpayer funds will be needed to pay for the added unemployment claims), and quite possibly as an employee (if he is unfortunate enough to be fired as a result of the added expenses to the company).

And finally, there is one more thing to be considered. The proponents of the fallacy mention increasing prices as a reason why more revenues are needed, but why are prices going up?

It should be obvious that taxes make things more expensive, but not just because the companies being taxed increase the prices of their goods and services to make up the difference. A much more insidious reason taxation makes everything more expensive is because the corporations who inevitably get the tax dollars increase the prices of their goods and services in response to the new Demand.

The reason for this is because, in transactions between a person and a business, the government is a 3rd party entity. If the government is buying goods and services on behalf of the public at large, this is Artificial Demand, i.e., Demand that wouldn't exist naturally. When Demand increases, assuming Supply remains the same or decreases, prices increase.

It should therefore be no surprise that prices are going up. Supply and Demand are not being left to operate naturally. Instead, they are being mechanically manipulated by people who can't possibly, no matter how many computers, scientists, or mathematical models they have, know the most efficient combination of Supply and Demand.

b. Taxes Create Jobs through Public Works

This is quite an old fallacy, and it is one that is easily smashed when you factor in what is not seen.

The line of thought goes like this. "We have unemployed people, who can't find jobs in the private sector. So therefore, we need public works in order to create jobs, which your tax dollars fund, and they will work to provide those services most vital to society as a whole."

Well, if those services are really so vital, then there's no reason to not consider them on that basis alone and not on the basis on job creation. Indeed, the people working in the public sector will do their duty, collect their salary, and then they will spend in the private sector for goods and services. This is true as stated. The problem is, what would the citizens do with their money had they not been taxed?

Just as in the case of the Broken Window Fallacy, you have the same opportunities created without the taxation. The jobs that were created through tax dollars, could be and would have been created in the private sector. The only difference is that they would've been different types of jobs in different sectors of the economy. Once we consider what is seen and what is unseen, we see quite clearly that taxation doesn't create jobs. The best taxation can do is shuffle jobs around.

c. Tax Cuts Hurt the Economy

This fallacy stems from the exact same place as the last one, and is put forth by the exact same people. The only difference is the line of thought, which goes like this, "If we cut taxes, we must lay off workers, who will no longer be able to provide the services vital to society. Also, they will not have a disposable income to spend in the private sector, and this will hurt businesses as a whole!"

It is true that if you cut taxes, you would have to lay off public workers, and that their income would be absent from private spending for a time. The problem is, where were public workers getting their salaries? They got it from tax dollars, which came from private individuals to begin with. The money that the private individual saves from not being taxed is money that he can spend in the private sector, invest in stocks and bonds, or set aside as savings.

This is a clear case of what is seen and what is not seen.

d. Public Officials and Employees Pay Taxes

This is an easy myth to explode, so I won't spend too much time on it.

Suppose you have a public employee (in any field you like) making a gross salary (salary before taxation) of $50,000. After taxes are taken out, he is left with a net salary of $35,000. So you would be inclined to say, "That person paid $15,000 in taxes."

Here's the problem; the source of his income is taxation. This means that he didn't actually pay $15,000 in taxes, but in fact collected $35,000 in tax dollars. His employment is a drain of $35,000 in tax dollars from the government, which may/may not be necessary. I'm not dealing with that right now. I'm dealing with the myth that public employees pay taxes.

Public employees, due to the nature of their income, therefore, can't pay taxes. They aren't tax payers, they are tax collectors.

e. Protective Tariffs are Necessary

You run into this fallacy a lot, mainly from businessmen facing foreign competition as well as politicians who either sincerely believe that domestic business needs protection, or are trying to appeal to the business tycoons in order to get campaign funding.

The case for Protectionism generally goes like this; "Foreign labor doesn't operate like our labor. They work like slaves, and as a result of their overtime and their very low wages, as well as their currency manipulation, their products are cheaper than ours. This causes our business to go overseas to other countries, and thus creates unemployment here at home. Therefore, it is necessary to have an equalizer in place so that competition isn't so unfair, and gives us a better chance in the world market."

So, let's take for example, an entrepreneur who makes Semi-Conductors, and sells them at $1,000 per Semi-Conductor. He has a competitor who, once the currency is converted over to dollars, and his expenses are paid, is able to sell essentially the same Semi-Conductor at $750 and still make a profit. This makes our entrepreneur very mad, since he knows he can't compete head-to-head with this foreigner. So, he petitions the government with the following case; "I am losing X amount as a result of this competition. In order to stay in business, I ask that tariffs be placed on my competitor. Then, those in the business to purchase Semi-Conductors would buy mine. I would then be in a position to raise my prices. That extra revenue will then go to increasing the wages of my workers, who will then spend this extra money elsewhere, and as a result, the standard of living of our country in general will increase."

The politicians, eager to have some statistics he can throw back to his supporters, as well as very generous campaign donations from the entrepreneur, grants the entrepreneur's oh-so-desperate plea for help against the relentless brutality of Market-Competition, and places protective tariffs on the foreign competitor's Semi-Conductors.

Now, this is a clear case of what is seen and what is not seen. What is seen is that, yes the entrepreneur will gain extra business from those in the market for Semi-Conductors, and yes he'll raise his prices, (for the sake of the example, we'll assume that he increased his price from $1,000 to $1,250). This is all true as stated, but there are problems in all of this that are not readily apparent. First, those who bought Semi-Conductors for $750 instead of $1,000 had a second buying opportunity with the $250 saved. This could've been invested back into their business, or set aside as savings to be invested later.

This extra investing would've created opportunities for other businesses and entrepreneurs. But, since the tariffs are in effect, those who are in the market for Semi-

Conductors not only forfeit the $250 buying opportunity that they would've had without the tariffs, they are losing an additional $250 as a result of the tariffs.

Thus, those who are in the market for Semi-Conductors are suffering a loss of $500 with each purchase of these propped up Semi-Conductors. This added expense is balanced out by laying off workers and/or raising prices, which ripples the same reaction throughout the economy, displacing productive labor and creating unemployment and a general lower standard of living for all parties involved except those who're directly being protected from competition.

Oh, and that promise the entrepreneur made of raising the wages of workers? Yeah... forget that. He pockets the extra profit, and politicians now have a huge incentive for keeping those protectionist tariffs in place. This sets the stage for more special favors down the road, with campaign funding and endorsements being primary motives for politicians to bid for the protected party's favor. This is a clear case of what is seen and what is not seen. Protectionist Tariffs should be avoided like the plague that they are.

Immigration

Immigration is a high-emotion issue, especially in the southern parts of the United States. Absolutely no one is satisfied with immigration in the United States. Complaints range from illegal immigrants taking our jobs (a fallacy dealt with in the following pages), to the influx of immigration adding to crime, to illegal immigrants getting welfare in the form of Social Security, food stamps, free public education, and free emergency-medical care, to immigration being too heavily regulated, etc. Due to the heavy emotions of this topic, it is very hard to deal with it both thoroughly and objectively, and even more so in a work of this nature.

Nevertheless, I shall try my best to correct the biggest of the economic fallacies concerning immigration.

a. "Dem illegals are takin' our jobs!!!"

This is a very typical outcry of your Mainstream Republican. The fallacy goes like this. "The illegals are pouring in by the thousands, and because they're willing to work for borderline slave wages, hard-working Americans are getting fired and replaced by illegal aliens who aren't even willing to learn the language!"

I won't deal with whether or not "illegals" are willing to learn the language, I'll simply point out that the Mainstream Republican position is riddled with severe internal contradictions, and this is one of them. Your typical Mainstream Republican will pay lip-service to the free-market whenever they get the chance, but it is very clear that they don't actually believe in the free-market, especially when it comes to immigration.

The reason for this is fairly straight-forward; they're Nationalists. They have some vague, arbitrary concept of what is "American", and they denounce everything that doesn't fall within this paradigm. But their paradigm is just that; vague and arbitrary. If asked, they would proudly say the Free-Market is as American as Baseball, Hotdogs, and Apple-pie.

Of course, their devotion to Nationalism prevents them from seeing that absolutely none of the above things they'd proudly list as being American originated in America, but there is a much more pressing issue, and that is the idea that the Free-Market is American. In fact, the Free-Market is no more American than it is German, British, Chinese, African, Indian, or any other nationality you might could think of.

The Free-Market is a method of social cooperation centered on unhampered trade and private ownership of the means of production, and is entirely independent of nationality. The appeals to Nationalism are meant to stir the sense of Patriotism within the listeners, and to use this sense of Patriotism to appeal to the listener's emotions in order to justify the given party's agenda.

Are "illegals", as they are commonly called today (a term that I absolutely despise, hence the quotation marks), in fact taking jobs away from hard-working Americans? Not at all. The immigrants who cross the border illegally are unskilled workers, and the primary bulk of "illegal" hiring is in areas that require unskilled labor, while the great bulk of American labor is skilled labor. The jobs that the immigrants are getting are jobs that hardly anyone would take because the wages are too low for him, or they consider the work to be too demeaning. It is very important to note that Mainstream Republicans are very quick to concede that the existence of Minimum Wage regulations provides a huge incentive for companies to hire "illegals."

If not for the labor of "illegal" immigrants, because they're willing to work for such low wages, we would have to pay much more for goods and services if we had instead hired American labor. To illustrate, let's consider a hypothetical.

Suppose you have a company of 1,000 workers making $12 per hour (they will not work for less, under any circumstances) working typical 8 hour shifts 5 days per week, in order to create a product that sells for $200 per unit. Just for the sake of simplicity, if we exclude the cost of materials, rent, and utilities such as electricity and water (I'm trying to focus strictly on labor here), then if you crunch the numbers, the factory will have to sell 115,200 units of that product at $200 just to cover the salaries being paid out to the workers (excluding payroll, and other taxes/benefits).

Here's how I'm getting that number.

The worker is making $12 per hour working an 8 hour shift, so 12 x 8 = 96. The worker is making $96 per day. The worker is working 5 days per week, so 96 x 5 = 480. The worker is making $480 per week. There are 4 weeks in a month, so 480 x 4 = 1,920. The worker is making $1,920 per month. Of course, there are 12 months in a year, so 1,920 x 12 = 23,040. The worker is making $23,040 per year.

There are 1,000 other workers making the same salary, so 23,040 x 1,000 = 23,040,000. It costs the company no less than $23,040,000 to employ the workers needed to make the product in question, but how many units of the product will the company have to sell at $200 in order to just cover this base cost of labor? 23,040,000/200 = 115,200. The company will have to sell no less than 115,200 units of the product at $200 per unit just to cover the base cost of labor. When payroll, utilities, adherence to government regulations, and other factors are thrown in, the company is clearly losing money if it only sells 115,200 units of the product in question.

But, if instead of paying workers $12 per hour, the company could instead pay its workers $8 per hour, the situation changes drastically. If wages drop from $12 per hour to $8 per hour, the company can drop the price of the product it's selling from $200 to $170. Using the same method as before, we can conclude that the company would need to sell, rounded up to the nearest one, 90,353 units of said product at $170 in order to cover the base cost of labor.

Or if they lowered even further to $150, then using the same method as before, we can conclude that the company would have to sell no less than 102,400 units of the product in question in order to cover the base salaries that the company is paying out.

It is important to note that it is much easier to sell a product for $170 or $150 than it is to sell the same product for $200. The company, thanks to being able to cut the price of their product, are much more likely to be successful in selling the product than they would be had they still priced it at $200 per unit, and thus, much more likely to make the profits they need to make.

The consumer at large benefits as well. The consumer who is in the market for this product has a second buying opportunity with the $30 or $50 saved. This second buying opportunity provides employment opportunities for other businesses and firms. But, in order for the consumers at large to reap these benefits, the price of labor at the company in question must fall.

I'm going to anticipate a criticism of this in advance, and point out that the neighboring businesses will not be hurt by the wages at the company dropping from $12 to $8 per hour. The price of consumer goods and services adjust themselves to the wages of the people at large, or as I explained earlier, Supply and Demand adjust themselves to each other.

There is also one other criticism of this that the Mainstream Republican might have at the ready; "In order for the company in your example to drop wages from $12 per hour to $8 per hour, assuming the workers in your example (as you yourself said) aren't willing to work for any less than $12, then the only way the company could possibly cut wages is if they fired all of the workers and replaced them. If they replaced them with illegals, then that is 1,000 hard-working Americans unemployed as a result of this cheap labor, which shouldn't be here to begin with! This can hardly be justified!"

Actually, it is more than justifiable, and it is justifiable in the same manner as labor-saving machines are justifiable. The added savings from decreased labor costs and lower consumer prices creates opportunities that would otherwise not existence. Now, granted, the 1,000 would be unemployed for a time, but as I pointed out in an earlier part of the book, idle resources are absolutely essential for the market to function.

The hiring of "illegals" (an act that next to no one would commit if they could purchase the labor of the citizens at large cheaper or as cheaply) is a signal from the market telling you that the price of a given part of the labor force, for whatever reason, is too high. The hiring of "illegals", thus, allows the labor which was displaced to flow into other sections of the economy where they will undeniably be more productive, and only someone who does not acknowledge the productivity of an unhampered division of labor would be opposed to that.

When you consider the poverty and the oppression that the so-called "illegal" immigrants lived in, and the sheer hell they went through in order to get here and find employment, then it becomes readily apparent that there is no other conclusion that can possibly be made than the conclusion that the immigrant who comes here "illegally" in order to work and provide for his family should be considered as nothing less than a hero; a shining example to the rest of the people at large, and we owe to him an incalculable debt.

What the Mainstream Republicans are really arguing for when they call for mass deportation of "illegals" on the basis that "illegals" are taking our jobs, is nothing more than an ugly form of Protectionism (covered in another section of this book), and justified by emotional arguments advocating some arbitrary notion of American values.

When this is examined closely, we see quite clearly that the Mainstream Republican believes neither in the Free-Market, nor in the unhampered division of labor.

War

War is a highly emotional issue among voters, especially Patriots/Nationalists and people who have relatives in the Military. When war does grace ourselves with its ugly presence, the flag is flown, the National Anthem is played, and the people at large take part in the patriotic show that follows. The media itself never truly questions the war, and only condemns the war when it is backed into a corner by cold, undeniable facts. An example of this is the recent war in Iraq.

From 2002-2003, the media blacklisted all criticisms of the Iraq War. Phil Donahue, a very popular pundit at MSNBC (in fact the host of the highest rated show on MSNBC at the time), had his show cancelled because he refused to support the Iraq War.[5]

NBC is considered by many to be nothing more than a cesspool of "Liberal, left-wing propaganda" in the media, and yet Phil Donahue was considered to be, by that same cesspool, "a tired, left-wing liberal out of touch with the current marketplace."

Bill Maher, a pundit/comedian, had his show, "Politically Incorrect" cancelled for going against the official script which called the terrorists who committed 9/11, "cowards." Bill Maher disputed this claim, and for his trouble, he had the White House Press Secretary Ari

Fleischer denounce him by saying, "people have to watch what they say and watch what they do."

You know, at first glance, this statement almost seems threatening... anyway.

Now, the Iraq War is widely viewed as a total failure by almost everyone, with the Mainstream Republican who views the Iraq War to be a huge success being the only exception. The reason being because the facts of the Iraq War are now undeniable to anyone who looks at that war objectively. Only die-hard Nationalists would deny the scandals of the Iraq War.

Nevertheless, with every single war, you can always count on there being someone saying that the war stimulates the economy and creates jobs. This is tied to the broken window fallacy (covered earlier in the book), but war has other disastrous effects on the economy, and the division of labor.

For starters, a war with country A sharply discourages business investment from country B if country B has some sort of alliance with country A. Business investment from country B would create tensions with country A, and unless country B is willing to risk breaking the alliance with country A, country B won't invest in the country at war with country A. It is considering this that we see a serious problem.

War strongly discourages foreign investment from specific countries. Although these days war isn't as simple as it once was, where it was one country against another each bearing their banner against another country, war nonetheless has the same effect.

Aside from the mass destruction and loss of life war brings, war also diverts production to things that are not beneficial to the economy, but destructive. As more money is spent by the government on drones, tanks, fighter jets, bombs, soldier recruiting, etc., more money is spent by private investors on projects that supplement these things.

The money that is spent by private investors on things that supplement instruments of war is money that can't be spent by investing in a car company to modernize its equipment, or invested in a farm so that the farm can hire more workers, etc.

Production is thus shifted in a way away from the direct wants/needs of the consumer, and more to the whims of the government and to the whims of Big Business Tycoons who know just where to invest for the greatest return. Then all of a sudden, it happens; business becomes so invested into war, it is in the business' interest to keep the war going. A couple of back-door deals with some very influential politicians, and voila! You now have a giant, corporatist machine hell-bent on waging war whenever and wherever they can sell war to the voters.

The Iraq War benefitted no one but a select few, and of that select few, Haliburton comes to mine. Is it any coincidence that Vice President Dick Cheney, former CEO of Haliburton, lobbied hard for the war in Iraq, and that Haliburton through KBR, got billions in government contracts to help manage the occupation of Iraq? I leave that for you to decide.

It must be remembered that appeals to Patriotism/Nationalism will never justify any action of war, nor is it a sufficient cover to avoid skepticism. Time itself reveals such tactics of deception as just that; tactics of deception.

War is not good for anyone, except for governments looking to expand their reach, weapon dealers looking to tap into the public funds, and large investors who not only have enough information to know exactly where to invest, but with enough capital to influence public policy.

War is, without a doubt, the fastest track to corruption that one can take, but one day people will realize that they themselves would be more than willing to trade, and possibly be friends with people abroad if they were allowed by the powers that be to have free, unhampered trade.

On the Subject of Market Failures

There are a myriad of things listed under the heading of "Market Failures." I've heard many definitions of the term Market Failure, but just for the sake of simplicity, I'll use this definition which I grabbed from Wikipedia.

"**Market failure** is a concept within economic theory describing when the allocation of goods and services by a free market is not efficient. That is, there exists another conceivable outcome where a market participant may be made better-off without making someone else worse-off."

There are many issues which people consider to be market failures, including but not limited to, negative/positive externalities (pollution is a prime example of a negative externality, and a new park that consequently increases property values is an example of a positive externality), lack of a "living wage", poor working conditions, just to name a few.

For the sake of simplicity, I won't be dealing with externalities in this book. The reason is because, in a work of this nature, I couldn't do the topic justice. Instead, if you want to learn about externalities, I refer you to the lectures given by Professor Walter Block on the subject of Market Failures. You can find them on YouTube.

Instead, I shall deal simply with what I consider to be the biggest so-called Market Failure that, more than anything else, is the driving force behind one of the most destructive policies that has ever been passed.

a. The Market Can't Provide a Livable Wage

This fallacy is huge, both in its implications, and its impact on the emotions of the people themselves. Let me pause for a moment by saying that once a fallacy has reached a person emotionally, it's almost impossible to correct. The person who believes in this fallacy emotionally is usually so far gone rationally that he won't listen to any sort of reason, no matter how well founded it is or how much empirical proof is behind it. He is, as the Holy Qur'an says, "Deaf, Dumb, and Blind."

The fallacy goes like this; "Corporations don't care about their workers. They care about making as much profit as they can, and the only way they can do this is by paying labor less than their worth.

Therefore, we need the Government to look after the public interest by making sure that the workers are receiving a wage that enables them to support themselves and their families."

This fallacy is problematic because it is built on half-truths, and all that is needed is an appeal to emotions to cover for the argument's deficiencies. The nugget of truth is that businesses and firms are only interested in making as much of a profit as they can make. They are, excluding a few exceptions, not driven by altruistic ideals such as the greater good of society.

But, is this in itself a bad thing? People are generally very skeptical of profit motives in and of themselves, and this is problematic because profit, which is purely subjective, governs the vast majority of all of our decisions as human beings.

Secondly, what is a livable wage, exactly? I've been given to understand that a livable wage is a wage that is absolutely necessary for workers to support themselves and their family, but this is a redundancy because that is exactly what the worker is getting for his services rendered anyway, without such things as minimum wage (I'll be dealing with that in detail here in a bit).

"How can that be when corporations only care about making a profit!?" I hear you say in a voice dripping with righteous indignation.

Because, corporations and entrepreneurs take into account the purchasing power of the people at large before pricing their final products. They want to satisfy as many customers as they can, but how can they do that when hardly anyone can afford the goods/services the corporations or the entrepreneur is offering?

They can't, which is why, as I mentioned before, big business, by the very nature of its being, serves the many. Because of this, the prices of goods and services adjust themselves to the wages of the people at large. If the entrepreneur or the corporation has overpriced their goods/services, the people at large will show them as much, and they will show them in a way that the entrepreneur or the corporation can't ignore; they will refuse to buy the goods/services at the prices that they're being offered. It is at this moment that the entrepreneur or the corporation must change its act, or they will go bankrupt.

It is also important to mention that, without a special contract, entrepreneurs and corporations don't own the labor of the workers, the workers own their labor. They are selling it to the corporations for the price agreed upon. If the workers aren't profiting off of their labor (profit is purely subjective), that is no one's fault, in a society free of coercive slavery, except for the worker who is selling his labor at the price that he is currently selling it. It is therefore up to the worker to find some way to make his labor more profitable to himself. He can collectively bargain with his boss, he could make his labor more efficient than the others and receive a promotion, he could change his profession, or he could seek employment elsewhere.

All of this is assuming that the division of labor is unhampered and that corporations are not protected from competition through government regulation.

b. Minimum Wage

This shall be the last fallacy I cover in this book (See, I told you that the title "Little Book" fits).

This spawns as a policy prescription due to the Livable Wage fallacy covered above. Minimum Wage is believed to be a step in the right direction at reducing income inequality and providing a better standard of living for workers, but this is not true. Let's say for example that the typical workers at a plant of 300 employees make $5 per hour. The employees all work 8 hour shifts for 5 days a week and are off on weekends. Excluding payroll and other taxes and benefits, the employer of these 300 employees can expect no less than $2,880,000 per year in labor costs.

Let's closely examine the math.

1 employee working an 8 hour shift 5 days a week at $5 per hour. So, 8 x 5 = 40. So the employee is making $40 a day. He works 5 days a week, so, 40 x 5 = 200. So he's making $200 a week. There are 4 weeks in a month, so, 200 x 4 = 800. Therefore, the employee is making $800 per month. There are 12 months in a year, so, 800 x 12 = 9,600. We can see that, excluding taxes, the employee makes $9,600 a year. There are 300 employees making $5 an hour, working the same hours, so, 9,600 x 300 = $2,880,000. We can see quite clearly that, to employ 300 men at $5 per hour for 5 days a week at 8 hour shifts, it will cost the employer no less than $2,880,000 per year,

and this number rises when you factor in taxes and other expenses.

Well, suppose some politician decides that this is unfair. He, in his righteous indignation, calls for a Minimum Wage of $7.50 per hour. The workers themselves, blinded by their personal interests and the smooth tongue of the politician, join in his call, and soon it is passed.

Now, let's rerun the numbers.

Now, the same employee is making $7.50 an hour working an 8 hour shift. 7.50 x 8 = 60. He is making $60 per day. He's still working 5 days a week, so, 60 x 5 = 300. Now, he is making $300 a week instead of $200 a week. There are 4 weeks in a month, so 300 x 4 = 1,200. The employee is thus making $1,200 per month, as opposed to the $800 per month he was making at $5 per hour.

There are 12 months in a year, so 1,200 x 12 = 14,400. So, just from increasing his hourly wage by $2.50, he gained $4,800 in yearly income.

And of course, there are 299 other employees making the exact same yearly wage, so, 14,400 x 300 = 4,320,000. So, instead of paying the $2,880,000 per year in salaries that he was paying before, he is now paying out no less than $4,320,000 in labor costs, and again, this is not counting taxes and other expenses. This is just the salary that the employer is paying out. **This is a 50% increase in labor**

expenses! But, does the entrepreneur directly pay this added expense? Not at all.

In fact. There is a very good chance that, to keep his expenses at or around the original $2,880,000 per year, he's going to fire workers. At 250 employees, the yearly expense decreases from $4,320,000 to $3,600,000, and at 200 employees, the yearly expense decreases back to the original yearly expense of $2,880,000.

This means that, assuming the employer doesn't increase the prices of his goods and services to mitigate the added labor expense, **you've paved the way through the Minimum Wage policy for up to 1/3rd of the labor force at this plant to be laid off! And of course, all of the people laid off are going to be filing for unemployment, which will cost the tax payers even more!**

It should be obvious from all of this that the increase in monetary income through Minimum Wage is merely a meaningless statistic. This added income comes at a very severe cost, which utterly destroys any sort of benefit you could derive from it.

But, to drive this point home further, let's take the extreme Minimum Wage proposal. To be more specific, the one that Occupy Wallstreet put forth to raise the Minimum Wage to $20 an hour.

Let's closely examine the math at our plant of 300 workers again.

The worker works in 8 hour shifts, so 20 x 8 = 160. It costs $160 a day to employ this worker.

He works 5 days a week, so 5 x 160 = 800. It now costs $800 a week to employ one worker. There are 4 weeks in one month, so 4 x 800 = 3,200. It costs the employer $3,200 a month to employ one worker.

There are 12 months in a year, so 12 x 3,200 = 38,400. So, to employ one worker for a year at $20 per hour Minimum Wage, the employer can expect no less than $38,400 in labor expenses. And of course, there are 299 other employees making the same Minimum Wage, so 38,400 x 300 = 11,520,000. So, to employ 300 workers for one year to work for 5 days a week at 8 hour shifts, **it will cost no less than $11,520,000 if the Minimum Wage goes up to $20 per hour!**

Only a fool could think that something such as this is feasible. This company would effectively be put out of business, because there is no way they could pass this expense onto the consumer/taxpayer.

In Conclusion

I hope I helped you, the average man, better equip yourself against economic myths and fallacies with this work. It is extremely brief, but the purpose of this simple work can't be satisfied in any other way.

I apologize to any professors who may be reading this for its simplicity and its brevity, but it was absolutely necessary, I assure you. Our future hinges on the average man, and without him, we have nothing but hopeless dreams and meaningless pontification, and quite frankly, we have enough of that as it is.

One only needs to turn on a mainstream cable news show to see it in its purest form. Listening to these people is the equivalent of listening to white-noise on your television screen, especially when the arguments become emotional, and they frequently do.

But, maybe, just maybe, this work can be a subtle step away from all of the fallacies hidden within the false complexities and toxic emotions created by professional propagandists.

To those who denounce this work due to its simplicity, I have only this to say; "Simplicity is the highest form of Complexity."

References

[1] Quotation taken from "Human Action: A Treatise on Economics" p. 874

[2] Quotation taken from Henry Hazlitt's "The Failure of the 'New Economics'"

[3] It is believed by many that Say's Law has been discredited by John Maynard Keynes. For more reading on this, see Henry Hazlitt's book, "The Failure of the 'New Economics'"

[4] Fact Check: The Wealthy Already Pay more Taxes by Stephen Ohlemacher

[5] MediaMatters for America, 10/29/04